THE MEDIEVAL CHURCH

Jessica Saraga

B. T. Batsford Ltd, London

CONTENTS

© Jessica Saraga 1994

First published 1994

Typeset by Goodfellow & Egan, Ltd, Cambridge

and printed in Hong Kong

Published by
B. T. Batsford Ltd
4 Fitzhardinge Street
London W1H 0AH

A CIP catalogue record for this book is available from the British Library.

ISBN 0 7134 6351 1

Cover illustration: An altar painting of Saints John the Baptist, Scholastica and Benedict, by an artist known as the Master of Liesborn. (Liesborn was the German town where the altar was originally painted in 1465.) Reproduced courtesy of the National Gallery.

Frontispiece: The Wilton Diptych (a diptych is a painting on two panels which are hinged like a book). Painted in the late fourteenth century, it shows Richard II of England being presented to the Virgin Mary by his patron saint.

Hearing the word 'church' today makes most people think of a building. People go to services there on Sundays, but for the rest of the week the buildings are usually much quieter. If you don't normally go to church yourself, you may wonder what reasons there are for learning about the medieval church.

There are churches in all the towns in Great Britain and most villages. Some village churches seem very big and imposing for just a small village, and sometimes you see a church which is all by itself in the countryside, not in a village at all. These churches are probably quite old, built in areas which used to be well populated but are not any more. Perhaps the population moved away into the towns many centuries ago.

If you go inside old churches you will probably find that a great deal of money was spent on building and decorating them. They might have massive stone pillars and window frames, carefully carved. Wood, also carved, may have been used extensively too. There may be stained glass windows with elaborate coloured patterns or pictures in them. Stone, wood and glass have always been expensive materials, and you may wonder who paid for all the building in these churches, where they got the money from, and why they chose to spend their money on a church rather than on themselves. As you read this book, you will find out that, in more than one sense, these people felt that they *were* spending their money on themselves.

As you look around a church, you may find some clues about the people who spent money on it. In many churches there are tombs where people have been buried, or plaques in the floor or the wall which commemorate their life and death. You may well have walked through a graveyard with hundreds more inscriptions on the tombstones. If so many people wanted to be buried in and around the church, they must have attached considerable importance to it.

You may deduce that these people must have been more religious than many people are today. Although today only a minority of people are particularly religious in this country, in the Middle Ages, or medieval period (which are terms used for the time roughly 500 to 1000 years ago), virtually everybody was religious. And although in twentieth century Europe people believe in a number of religions including Christianity, Hinduism, Islam, and Judaism, in medieval Europe the overwhelmingly dominant religion was Christianity. Christianity split into only two kinds: orthodox Christianity in Eastern Europe, and Catholicism in Western Europe. There were no separate churches of England or Scotland, and no Methodists, Baptists, Quakers, Jehovah's Witnesses or other forms of Christianity that exist now.

So when we talk about 'The Medieval Church', we are not just referring to buildings, but to the whole religious system of Christianity – its beliefs, customs, and since it was rich and powerful, the way it controlled people's lives too. It may be becoming clear to you already that the medieval church could be an important area of study. If you are not a religious person yourself, try to understand medieval people who had beliefs that you don't share. If you had been alive then, you almost certainly would have believed as they did. If you are a religious person, whatever your religion, it should be interesting to compare your own experience of the way religious influences operate on you, with what you find out about the way the Catholic church influenced people's ideas and lives in the Middle Ages.

Introductory quiz

Do you know?

What the Old and New Testaments are?

The story of St Francis of Assisi?

The difference between a monk and a friar?

Which Spanish town is associated with St James?

What a Mystery Play is?

Which saint medieval Christians believed looks after travellers?

Which English writer wrote a long poem about pilgrims?

THE CATHOLIC CHURCH

All of the older churches in this country were once Catholic churches, though few of them are so now. The majority are now Protestant churches. But they still provide many clues about the beliefs of the medieval Catholics who built them and worshipped in them. If you were transported back in time and were able to go inside a medieval church building soon after it was built, you would find even more. And you would find something in the church relevant to all stages of life from birth to death.

In the following paragraphs, I am going to write about Christianity in the past tense, even though it is still very much a living religion. This is because I want to emphasize that it is not twentieth century Christianity or twentieth century Catholicism which I am writing about, but medieval Christianity.

Christians believed in what is written in the Bible. Part of the Bible, the Old Testament, is a collection of the ancient Hebrew writings which are the basis of the Jewish faith. It tells stories about a single God, who made the universe. It tells how he created the world and all the life forms on it. The first man and woman, Adam and Eve, lived in the garden of Eden, where there was no sin. But Adam and Eve disobeyed the rule God had made that they should not eat the fruit of a tree described as the tree of the knowledge of good and evil. Their punishment for this disobedience was to be driven out of the garden. The picture here is from a medieval Bible, and shows how Adam and Eve were persuaded to eat the fruit by the Devil in the form of a snake. The other picture shows them leaving the garden. This episode is known as The Fall because Adam and Eve were thought to have fallen from goodness into sin.

The Old Testament also tells stories about the descendants of Adam and Eve, who are also called Hebrews, Jews, Israelites, the children of Israel, or sometimes God's chosen people. There are stories about their leaders, such as Moses, and their *prophets* such as Isaiah. A prophet is someone who predicts what will happen in the future. One of the most famous *prophecies* (predictions) in the Old Testament, is that one day a boy would be born who would save the Jews from all their enemies, and become their leader. He would be called the Messiah.

(Left) The fifteenth century Italian artist Masaccio shows the remorse and despair of Adam and Eve as they leave the garden of Eden.

(Right) Adam, Eve and the Devil in the form of a snake with a human head, from a thirteenth century Northern French Bible.

Up to this point, Christian and Jewish beliefs are very similar. However, disagreement arose about two thousand years ago when Jesus of Nazareth claimed to be the long-awaited Messiah. Some Jews believed him; others regarded him as just another prophet. The first Christians were those Jews who did believe Jesus was the Messiah, and that he was both man and God. The word 'Christian' comes from 'Christ', another word for Messiah.

The New Testament of the Bible contains the Gospels (meaning 'good news'), written by Matthew, Mark, Luke and John. The Gospels describe Jesus' birth, his life of teaching and healing, his death by execution, and the attempts by the early Christians to persuade people that their view of Jesus was the correct one. After Jesus died, his followers set about spreading Christianity. One of them, St Peter, assumed authority over all Christians. He was called the *Pope* (a word meaning 'father'), or the Bishop of Rome. Throughout the medieval period, later Popes exercised control over the church, with a growing network of bishops and priests to administer it. The Popes had authority in religious matters over all the Christian people in Europe, including kings and other rulers. For people in Christian areas there was no question of whether or not to be a Christian; simply by being born you were part of the Church.

Children were also received formally into the church by being baptized, or christened. Baptism was one of seven *sacraments*, which were practices symbolizing the *grace* (help) by which God enabled people to overcome the sinfulness they had inherited from Adam. The other sacraments were *confirmation*, when people repeated for themselves the promises made for them at baptism by their godparents; marriage; preparation for death; *ordination* (becoming a priest); *absolution* (when people received forgiveness for their sins after confessing to a priest); and perhaps most important of all, the *Mass*. This was a church service in which bread and wine were said to become the body and blood of Jesus. It was also a reminder of the Last Supper eaten by Jesus and his disciples before Jesus was arrested.

The Seven Sacraments

As you can see from the painting below, the priest played an important role in administering the sacraments. There is a priest baptizing a baby, hearing confession, holding up the symbol of Christ's body in the Mass, performing a wedding, and ministering to a dying man. Confirmation and ordination are performed by bishops, recognizable by their *mitre* (a pointed double hat). So priests were familiar and important figures to Christians at all the various stages of life. You can also see in the painting various reminders of Christian beliefs; the *font*, in which babies were baptized, the *altar* (holy table) on which Mass was celebrated, and above the altar a statue of Mary the mother of Jesus, with her baby. The crucifixion scene in the foreground is not a part of the church, but this whole painting was designed to be displayed in a church, above the altar, and was itself therefore a reminder to people of many different aspects of their religion. How many angels can you see shown in the picture below? What is your definition of an angel?

Look at the clothes worn by the people in the crucifixion scene in the picture, and in the other scenes which show the sacraments. How has the artist tried to indicate by clothing that the crucifixion took place nearly 1500 years before?

Rogier van der Weyden, The Seven Sacraments, *painted in the mid-fifteenth century.*

1 Find an old church to visit, dating if possible back to before the sixteenth century. Discuss with your teacher when to go and whether you might need to make arrangements to look inside. Look for the altar and the font, and see if you can find out where the bread and the wine are kept. (The Mass is called Holy Communion in the Church of England). Notice whether there are any memorials to the dead inside the church.

2 Using a modern translation of the Bible (such as the Good News Bible), start reading from the beginning (the Book of Genesis). You will find two stories about the Creation, followed by the story of Adam and Eve's disobedience to God. Do you think the artists who painted the pictures on pages 4 and 5 have illustrated the story of Adam and Eve successfully?

What do the following words mean?

Purgatory
prophet
ordination
font
mitre
altar

The Role of the Priest

Priests grew in importance as a new belief began to take hold in Christianity in the Middle Ages. This was the idea of *Purgatory*. Christians believed that souls survived even after the body was dead. People who had led good lives or who were truly sorry for their sins would go to heaven. But many people would die before being truly sorry, and would therefore have to suffer for a time in Purgatory before going to heaven. Those still alive could help to lessen their time in Purgatory by praying for them, or by having Masses said for them. Mass could only be said by a priest, who would often charge a fee.

The Message of God

Up to now God had been indignant with the human race because of the fault of the first parent, but now, seeing the Son become a man, He will no longer be angry.

(Anon, *Meditations on the Life of Christ*, 14th century, translated from the Latin by Ira Ragusa)

Writings like this were designed to underline the teachings of the Bible. Educated people could read them in Latin, and there were also translations into the main languages of Europe.

Rich people were often very careful to make a will before they died. How could they use their wills to try to lessen the time they would spend in Purgatory when they died? Was there anything a poor person could do to spend less time in Purgatory?

The names of the seven sacraments?
Who was the first Bishop of Rome (or Pope)?

What was the 'fault of the first parent?' Who do you think is meant by 'the first parent'? Would it have been fairer to say 'parents' instead of 'parent'?
Explain in your own words why the writer thinks God 'will no longer be angry'.

THE VIRGIN MARY

As Christianity grew and developed, Christian ideas changed too. One of the newer ideas in the early Middle Ages emphasized the particular importance of Mary the mother of Jesus. Jesus was believed to be the son of God, and so could not have a human father. Mary therefore was believed to have remained a virgin even after she became pregnant and gave birth to Jesus. Mary was also believed to be the only human being not to have inherited Adam's sinfulness.

Theologians (scholars who studied Christian teaching) said that because Mary was pure and free from sin, she went straight to heaven, body and soul, at the end of her life. She became queen of heaven, and sat at Christ's right hand. Her prayers from heaven were believed to be particularly effective in saving the souls of people in Purgatory (see page 7), and in relieving suffering on earth. Many people therefore prayed to Mary more often than they prayed to God.

There were stories about Mary saving people from death – even holding up a hanged man inside the noose – so that they would not die before they had a chance to repent. Another story tells of a certain Theophilus, who sold his soul to the devil, giving the devil an agreement written in his blood. When the time came for him to die, Theophilus repented, and Mary recovered his agreement and gave it back to him so that he could tear it up and prevent the devil from coming for his soul. Theophilus really lived in the sixth century, long after Mary died. This illustrates how more and more stories grew up about Mary which could not possibly have been true. Mary became a cult figure (someone who is widely famous and popular, like a singer or film actor today). You could also say that Mary was regarded by many people like a goddess, even though Christian teaching said that there was only one God, the Trinity of Father, Son and Holy Spirit.

Paintings and statues of Mary became very popular. The most common were those which portrayed Mary with the baby Jesus, often surrounded by angels. The nativity scenes with shepherds or the three kings which are familiar to us today became popular only in the late Middle Ages.

People who looked up to Mary as a perfect woman often compared her to Eve. She is even sometimes called the 'second Eve'. But where Eve was blamed for causing sin in the world by tempting Adam, Mary was praised for giving birth to Jesus, who would release humanity from sin. 'Mary is the bright eye that illuminates the world, Eve the other eye, blind and dark', wrote an early Christian, Ephrem of Syria, in the fourth century.

The comparison with Eve illustrates two extreme views of women held by the medieval church, and therefore by most medieval people in Europe. A woman was thought of either as an evil temptress who was to blame for everything that went wrong in the world, including the sins that men committed, or as a pure virgin who could put everything right.

It is important to remember that in the medieval church, sex was regarded as sinful even within marriage. If possible, it was thought, you should live without it. Priests and monks and nuns vowed that they would live chastely (without sex), but clearly the vow produced some tensions. 'Lord, make me chaste,' prayed Augustine, later to become a saint, 'but not yet'!

In blaming Eve for sin, men seemed to blame women for their own desires. It must have been hard for Christian women to be on the receiving end of these opinions, expressed by the authorities of the Christian faith. They were told that they were daughters of Eve, and were personally responsible for sin. But women could always turn to Mary for comfort and support, and ironically they could pray to her together with men. Her appeal cut across gender. One more charitable English medieval poet gave thanks for Adam and Eve and the fall because they made Mary possible:

> Never had the apple taken been,
> The apple taken been,
> Never had Our Lady
> Been heaven's queen
> Blessed be the time
> The apple taken was
> Therefore we must sing
> Deo gratias! [thanks to God]

The Coronation of the Virgin *of Giusto de' Menabuoi (fourteenth century) shows Mary dressed in white and gold as Queen of Heaven.*

THE VIRGIN MARY

The Virgin Birth – Two extracts from anonymous medieval poems

'Hail Mary, full of grace! And may Our Lord
Be with you!' was the angel Gabriel's word.
'The fruit of your womb, I declare, shall be blest;
You shall carry a child beneath your breast'.

This greeting and word which the angel had brought,
Mary considered and pondered in thought.
She said to the angel, 'How could such thing be?
Of knowledge of man my body is free'.

She was virgin with child, and virgin before,
And still virgin yet when her Baby she bore.
Never was maiden a mother but she;
Well might she the bearer of God's son be!

How could a woman be at once
A mother and a maiden pure,
And bring to birth a child without
A man defiling her?

She would not do a deed of wrong;
I trust her purity
I know and swear that this is so,
And found it so to be.

More likely is it that she would
Without a man conceive,
Than that she would gravely sin,
And Joseph so deceive.

From the evidence of these extracts, do you think medieval people found it easy to believe in the Virgin Birth (the idea that Mary had a baby without sex with a man)? The second extract is supposed to be Joseph speaking. How does he convince himself?

CHECK YOUR UNDERSTANDING

What is meant by the following?

theologian
cult figure
the Fall
chaste

The devil in the left of this woodcut is dressed in women's clothes, which illustrates the tendency in the Middle Ages to equate women with sinfulness.

A fifteenth century south German wood-cut of Mary as both mother and queen.

Mary's different roles

The church gave Mary more and more official titles – Mother of God, Everlasting Virgin, Queen of Heaven, Sorrowing Mother, Our Lady (or in French, Notre Dame and Italian, Madonna). She was also unofficially seen as the Bride of God, the Star of the Sea who protected sailors, and the Moon – which traditionally as with the Greek goddess Artemis, had associations with both chastity and fertility. With her associations with the sky and sea, her colour was blue and you almost always see her in paintings wearing a blue cloak, though sometimes she has on underneath the red robe of a queen or sometimes the white of a virgin. Perhaps the most enduringly popular idea of Mary though is of the young mother with her baby, as illustrated here.

Which of Mary's roles described above fits your own idea of her best?

CAN YOU REMEMBER ?

Why Mary in the story held up a hanged man inside the rope? How nativity scenes were shown in the early Middle Ages? Why Mary is usually shown wearing blue, red or white?

THINGS TO DO

1 In gender groups (either girls or boys, but not mixed), discuss whether there are any stereotypes (set ways of thinking) about women today, and whether they correspond to the medieval stereotypes of Mary the Virgin and Eve the Temptress. Make a list of the qualities which parallel stereotypes of Jesus and Adam would have.

2 Design a wall-hanging or panel for a medieval church illustrating one or all of Mary's roles. You can use words, drawing, symbols, or a combination of any of them.

3 Write a list of any twentieth century cult figures you have heard of. Include in the list why they are famous, and which countries they come from.

MONKS AND MONASTERIES

Most people know what monks and nuns are. Not everybody gives much thought, though, to the reasons why men and women might choose to become monks and nuns, which means giving up not just everything they own, but also sex and parenthood, and much of their freedom. In the Middle Ages, there was never a shortage of people wanting to do this. There were large numbers of monasteries and nunneries, which quite often had to turn away people who wanted to become monks and nuns, for lack of room.

Perhaps the most important thing to remember in trying to understand this is that people had no doubt that they would be severely punished for sin, both in their life on earth, and for ever afterwards in the torture of hell. The fear of this punishment made them want to try to avoid sin. Many people also felt a sincere emotional love of God, or more specifically of Mary, Jesus and the Christian saints. Because of this love, they wanted to live according to Christian principles, which they believed were right. If you wonder how people could feel love for something they could not see, or for people long since dead, you might make a comparison with the intense feelings people have today for singers or performers long since dead, whom they have only seen on the screen, such as Marilyn Monroe, James Dean, or Elvis Presley.

Some men and women felt that the only way they could truly do God's will and avoid sin was to retreat from all the distractions and temptations of the world, and concentrate on praying to God in the company of other likeminded individuals. Although it was hard for many of them to give up the

(Left) This illustration from a fifteenth century book of psalms shows monks in the choir stalls in church. How well are they all concentrating on their singing?

(Right) Fountains Abbey, founded in 1132, was the greatest of the Cistercian abbeys in Britain. It was the centre of a remarkable network of agriculture and industry.

company of the opposite sex, they believed in the ideal of *chastity* (living without sex). Some people responded positively to the ideal, and enjoyed living in a single sex environment.

People outside the monasteries were happy to support them for several reasons. First of all, they knew that the monks and nuns could be asked to pray for the sins of others, and do the *penance* (earthly punishment for sin) which busy people didn't have time for. After the Battle of Hastings in 1066, the Norman bishops said there must be a penance by the victorious army of one year's fasting for every Saxon they had killed. Without the completion of this penance, the soldiers' immortal souls would be in danger. However, both the bishops and the soldiers were happy to allow the penance to be done by monks, on payment of a suitable sum of money.

A second reason why the powerful families of Europe were willing to support monasteries and nunneries concerns the ownership of property. The wealth of these families was derived from the large estates they owned. They were reluctant to divide up the ownership of the land by splitting it between the children when the head of the family died, so they left the whole estate to the eldest son. Consequently many younger sons, and daughters for whom there was not enough land to inherit or provide a *dowry* (piece of land to give to her husband on marriage) would enter the monastic life. The families would see to it that the monasteries and nunneries were well provided for, so that their sons and daughters could live comfortably; sometimes they would even set up a monastery or nunnery just for their own family.

The first monasteries were set up in the sixth century by St Benedict. Monasticism was especially successful in Italy where St Benedict lived, because the monasteries and nunneries provided a safe refuge from the marauding armies which kept invading the country. St Benedict devised a set of rules which would help people live together in harmony and obedience to God. The accent was on self-discipline, but he did not want to impose rules that were too harsh and too difficult to keep, so he called his *Rule* (set of rules), written in the early sixth century, a 'very little rule for beginners'.

He was very insistent that there was to be no 'murmuring' against the rules, so where he thought they might prove hard, he built in some leeway.

For instance, after going to bed at nightfall, the monks had to get up at midnight for a service. St Benedict decided that the first *Psalm* (religious poem or song from the Bible) in this service must be said very slowly, so that anyone who had difficulty in getting out of bed could creep in not too late. St Benedict also said that the *abbot* (head) of each monastery must look after his monks in every way, particularly if they were ill.

The Benedictine monks became known as the black monks, because of the colour of their *habits* (distinctive religious dress). Later there were other orders of monks founded. One was the Augustinians, who wore brown, and became known for their emphasis on caring for the community. Another was the order of white monks, the Cistercians, who preferred to cut themselves off from society completely, and build their monasteries in remote areas. Their rules were very strict.

Ailred, Abbot of Rievaulx

He gave his frail body no pleasure at all in this earthly life. His bones could be clearly seen through his thin flesh and his lips seemed to frame his teeth. He ate scarcely anything and drank even less.

This description was written by Walter Daniel, one of the Cistercian monks at Rievaulx (in Yorkshire) in the twelfth century.

Compare this description of Abbot Ailred, who was a Cistercian monk, with the lifestyle of the Benedictine monks. What clue does it give about what pleasures Ailred must have been looking forward to in the future?

(Above right) A floor plan of Rievaulx Abbey.

The ruins of the Cistercian Abbey of Rievaulx, where Ailred lived (see above).

The Rule of St Benedict

Here are some extracts from St Benedict's 'very little rule for beginners'.

Whether the monks ought to have anything of their own
Let no-one presume to give or receive anything whatever for his own, neither book, nor tablets, nor pen, nor anything else.

The amount of food
We believe it to be sufficient for the daily meal, whether it be at the sixth or ninth hour, that every table have two cooked dishes, on account of the individual weaknesses of the brothers, so that he who, by chance, cannot eat out of the one, may eat from the other.

Of the daily manual labour
Idleness is the enemy of the soul. The brothers, therefore, ought to be engaged at certain times in manual labour, and at other hours in divine reading. After the sixth hour, let them rise from the table and rest on their beds in perfect silence. If anyone may wish to read to himself, let him do so in such a way as not to disturb the others. It is naturally of great importance that at these times when the brothers are free for reading, two senior brothers shall be assigned to go the rounds of the monastery and make sure that none of the brothers, from laziness, is spending his free time idly or in gossip.

The reception of guests
All guests who arrive at the monastery shall be received as Christ. The monks shall employ the greatest care and solicitude in the reception of poor people and pilgrims. Let none of the brothers associate or speak with the guests, unless they are specially instructed to do so.

What evidence is there here of St Benedict's desire not to make life so hard for the monks that they failed to keep the rules?

Compare the rules in this extract with your school rules. Is there anything that you are allowed to do while you are at school that the monks were forbidden?

CHECK YOUR UNDERSTANDING

What do the following words mean?

penance
dowry
abbot
psalm

CAN YOU REMEMBER ?

Why monasteries were so popular in medieval times? How rich families made sure their sons and daughters had a reasonable standard of living? What colour robes each of these monks wore: Benedictines, Augustinians, Cistercians.

THINGS TO DO

1 Using the evidence on pages 11–14, write down a list of rules for Benedictine monks, including both what they were forbidden to do, and what they were told they had to do.

2 Write an extract from the diary of a teenage novice (beginner) in either a Benedictine or Cistercian monastery, showing both hope to become a good monk and fear that it might be very hard. Which rules would be hardest to obey?

FRIARS AND NUNS

Although by the thirteenth century, the Benedictines, Augustinians, and Cistercians still existed, some of the monasteries were finding it hard to support large numbers of monks on the income from the land the monastery owned. Many of the monks became worried about the economic survival of their monasteries. Some monks were also concerned that life in the monasteries had got too far away from the simple ideals of Benedict and the other founders of monasticism.

It was because of this that two orders of friars were founded. Friars were groups of men who did without a home base in a monastery, and tried to lead a monastic life more economically in the outside world. One group was founded by Dominic, originally an Augustinian monk, who was also worried about *heresy* (beliefs which were different from the official beliefs of the Catholic church). He thought it was important to eliminate heresy from the church by persuading *heretics* (people who believed in heresy) that their ideas were wrong, and by setting an example of what to believe and how to live. He could only do this by living amongst ordinary people.

So in 1217 Dominic and his colleagues, probably at first less than 20 people, decided to travel separately through France and Spain, with Dominic himself going to Rome. Later Dominicans tried to combat heresy by their intellectual influence in the universities, which were the main centres of discussion about Christian ideas.

The second order of friars followed St Francis of Assisi (whose love of birds and animals you may have heard of). Francis was a rich young man, who became disgusted by wealth and material possessions. He emphasized that poverty was the way to God. Jesus had said that it was harder for a rich man to go to heaven than for a camel to get through the eye of a needle, which seemed to mean that unless people shared out all their wealth apart from what they needed to live, they could not get to heaven at all. Franciscans therefore depended on people's charity. People usually gave willingly to them, hoping this charitable act might help to save their immortal souls. Eventually people gave so much to them that they broke their own rules and built large churches and friaries to live in.

Meanwhile, women were also playing a part in the kind of religious life led by monks and friars. Women sometimes had their own reasons for wanting to retreat from the world to become nuns. Medieval women, particularly noble women, could not be independent of men because they had no way of supporting themselves financially. On becoming adult they would just move from the control of their father to the control of a husband. Life in a community of other women might seem a safe, civilized and attractive alternative. A nunnery was also a safe home to go to when a woman was widowed. Other women sincerely wanted to spend their lives in the service of God, and of the people outside the nunnery, for whom the nuns prayed. Praying was thought to be something at which women were particularly effective, so the nuns' prayers were in high demand.

When the first Benedictine monasteries were set up, there were several double monasteries with one house for men and one for women. Sometimes they were under the overall control of an abbess rather than an abbot. However, double monasteries did not survive long. One reason given by Conrad of Marchtal was that 'the wickedness of women is greater than all the wickedness of the world' and that 'the poison of vipers and dragons is more curable and less dangerous to men than the familiarity of women'. Bernard of Clairvaux put it more specifically: 'to be constantly in the company of a woman, and not to have intercourse with her is more difficult than to raise the dead'. The nuns apparently fell victim to the monks' inability to control themselves; they had to go.

But many women were still determined to be nuns. Benedictine nunneries survived, and later, Cistercian nunneries were set up. Cistercian monks tried to exert control over them, and limit their freedom, but the nuns were determined to be independent. Women who wanted to live like the wandering Franciscans also encountered male hostility. They set up an order called the Poor Clares, but the friars refused to collect *alms* (charity) for women. Altogether, it was very hard for women to live a religious life in a church whose official organization was dominated by unsympathetic men. Their survival is a tribute to their determination.

In Sansetta's early fifteenth century
painting you can see St Francis taking off
his fashionable cloak to give to a poor
barefoot knight. You can see him again
in bed dreaming about a fortress with
banners, a prophetic symbol of the order
of friars he has not yet founded.

FRIARS AND NUNS

The Beguines

One of the most successful women's orders was not really an order at all. The Beguines were women who just decided to leave their homes and live a religious life together. They had no one set of rules; some of them worked in the community and some of them didn't. Their main motive was to find a religious life which suited themselves. The word Beguine was a word for 'heretic', and was used as a smear on the women, but they did not let it affect them. The Beguines originated in the Netherlands, and in Cologne on the river Rhine in Germany. Their continuing popularity can be measured by the fact that there were still Beguines in Cologne at the end of the eighteenth century.

Teachings of St Francis

Praised be my Lord God with all his creatures, and specially our brother the sun, who brings us the day and who brings us the light. Praised be my Lord for our sister the moon, and for the stars, the which he has set clear and lovely in heaven. Praised be my Lord for our brother the wind, and for air and cloud, calms and all weather by the which thou upholdest life in all creatures. Praised be my Lord for our sister water, who is very serviceable unto us and humble and precious and clean. Praised be my Lord for our mother earth, the which doth sustain us and keep us, and bringeth forth divers fruits and flowers of many colours, and grass.

(From *the Song of the Sun*, by St Francis, early 13th century)

In 1274 the church authorities criticized the Beguines for having translations of the Bible in their own languages and discussing the bible with ordinary people in the street. Why do you think the church saw this as a threat?

The nun in this scene from a manuscript is receiving absolution (see page 5) from a Franciscan friar to whom she has confessed her sins.

How differently might St Francis express the ideas in this extract if he was a modern environmentalist or conservationist?

THINGS TO DO

1 Write a letter from a nun or a monk to the Pope, explaining your views on the merits of double monasteries.

2 Write a story, or strip cartoon, about someone today who, like St Francis, decides for religious reasons to give away everything he or she owns.

This fourteenth century woodcut shows a noble Spanish lady, Maria de Molina, authorizing some nuns to found a convent.

Rich Friars

The idea of a rich friar should have been a contradiction. These two extracts show the contrast between the ideal and the reality.

For there he was not like a cloisterer,
With a threadbare cope, as is a poor scholar,
But he was like a master or a pope.
Of double worsted was his semi-cope.

(A description of a friar from *The Canterbury Tales* by Geoffrey Chaucer)

The brothers shall take nothing for their own, neither a house, nor a place, nor anything at all. But like strangers and pilgrims in this life, serving God in poverty and humility, they shall go forth confidently to seek alms, not be ashamed to do so, since Our Lord made himself poor for us in this world.

(From *The Rule of St Francis*)

In the poem to the left, a cloisterer is a monk; a cope is a cloak. Worsted was an expensive woollen cloth.

THE CHURCH AND EDUCATION

In the early centuries after the death of Jesus, European scholars believed that the only purpose of learning was to understand more about God's purpose in the world. This must be done by understanding the complex layers of meaning in the books of the Bible, in which there was a great deal of *symbolism* (using one thing to stand for another), and *metaphor* (expressing your meaning in terms of something else). In order to be able to understand the symbols and metaphors, scholars believed they would need to study pre-Christian, *secular* (non-religious) works too, for example books about science and nature. So although not all learning was directly about religion, it was all designed for a

The monk Eadwine painted this self-portrait as an illustration for the Psalter (book of psalms) he wrote in Canterbury in the middle of the twelfth century.

religious purpose. Much of it developed into study of the meanings of words and ideas, which was known as *grammar*, and the study of how to use language to convey ideas to other people, which was known as *rhetoric*.

When monasteries became popular they developed into centres of learning for different reasons. First of all, the Rule of St Benedict had said that each monk must spend at least four hours a day studying, and choose a book every year at *Lent* (the 40 days of fasting just before Easter) for his year's reading. This in itself meant that there must be some scholarly monks who could read and write, to build up a library for the monastery by copying books out by hand. Some monks developed immense skill in *illumination* (the art of decorating manuscripts with pictures and designs).

There was also a need for learned monks to devise and write down the set services and prayers which were used, to write hymns, and compose and write down the music for hymns, *psalms* and services, which meant that they had to be educated. And with so many services to fit in to each day, starting with the one at midnight, there had to be a reliable way of telling the time, as they had no clocks. This meant that the monks had to develop a knowledge of astronomy so as to be able to tell the time by the stars. One monastery near Orleans in France wrote down instructions like this: 'On Christmas Day, when you see the Twins lying, as it were, on the dormitory, and Orion over the chapel of All Saints, prepare to ring the bell. And on 1 January, when the bright star in the knee of Artophilax is level with the space between the first and second window of the dormitory and lying as it were on the summit of the roof, then go and light the lamps.'

From about the eleventh century onwards a body of students grew up who were not directly connected with the church. Their desire for education created a demand for teachers, and it was the ability of certain teachers to draw students to them which created the nucleus for the development of universities. The teachers might teach *theology* (the study of religion), or they might teach law as in Bologna in Italy, or medicine as in another Italian town, Salerno.

A monk teaching. Note the candle used for reading after dark or in the poor light inside some buildings.

the church as a tax). From the beginning of the thirteenth century they could also become friars. The friars, particularly the Dominicans, were dedicated to learning; they devoted much of the income received in alms or *bequests* to supporting friars in their study at the universities.

Schools, too, were almost always controlled by the church. They would normally have to be licensed by the bishop of the area, who would make sure that he approved of the teachers (again almost always priests) who were appointed. Some of the schools were attached to cathedrals or churches.

So during much of the Middle Ages, all branches of learning were to some extent in the hands of the church. In England the church and the universities developed such strong links that as late as the sixteenth century, it was very unusual to study at university without becoming a priest. One effect of these close links was to increase the influence of the church over all areas of thought. All learning was Christian, and it was not possible to separate religious scholarship from scholarship in general.

An illuminated letter C showing the great skill of many monks and the typically bright colours they used to liven up the rows of text.

The universities were encouraged by rulers of the area, because they could see the value of having a body of men educated in logic or the law, who could be useful as political administrators or advisers.

But even though the universities had not started out with a connection with the church, they did develop one. Most of the students found it very hard to support themselves financially while they were studying, as many still do. If a student wanted to continue to study after obtaining a degree, almost the only way to do it was by becoming a priest, and thus receiving an income from rents or *tithes* (a tenth of people's produce which had to be paid to

THE CHURCH AND EDUCATION

At University in Paris

Read these extracts about university life in Paris, and answer the questions below:

No-one is to lecture in arts (literature as well as painting etc.) before he is twenty-one years old. He is to listen in arts at least six years, before he begins to lecture. No master lecturing in arts is to wear anything except a cope, round and black and reaching the heels – at least when it is new. He is not to wear under the round cope embroidered shoes, and never any with long bands.

We decide concerning the theologians, that no one shall lecture at Paris before he is thirty-five years old, and not unless he has studied at least eight years.

(Statutes of Robert de Courcon for Paris in 1215)

As to the doctors of theology, they were swollen with learning, but their charity was not edifying (did not provide a good example). They not only hated one another, but by their flatteries they enticed away the students of others; each one seeking his own glory, but not caring a whit about the welfare of souls. They sought the work decidedly less than the status. They were in such haste to become masters that most of them were not able to have any students, except by entreaties and payments.

(Jacques de Vitry, 13th century)

Which subject did Robert de Cour-con (who was a representative of the Pope) consider was the hardest to teach?

Why do you think the lecturers' copes (cloaks) might not reach to their heels once they were no longer new? Why shouldn't they wear 'embroidered shoes' and 'long bands'?

What evidence is there in the second extract that the doctors of theology were not good enough teachers to attract students?

This illuminated letter B comes from the Winchester Bible, which was made in the fourteenth century. It combines decoration with story-telling. What is going on inside the two parts of the B?

A fifteenth century drawing of the warden, monks and scholars of Winchester College, with the building in the background.

Schools in London

In London three principal churches have by privilege and ancient dignity, famous schools. On feast days the masters have festival meetings in the churches. Boys of different schools strive against one another in verses, and contend about the principles of grammar and rules of the past and future tenses.

(William Fitzstephen, *Description of the most Noble City of London*, 1173)

What modern television equivalents of these 'grammar matches' can you think of?

CHECK YOUR UNDERSTANDING

What do these words mean?

symbolism
secular
theology
tithe

CAN YOU REMEMBER ?

Why monks and nuns needed to be able to tell the time accurately?
What subjects were taught in medieval universities?
Why secular rulers encouraged universities?
How many hours a day Benedictine monks had to study?

THINGS TO DO

1 Copy out a short verse from the Bible and illuminate the first initial letter with coloured decoration in the way monks did.

2 Draw two cartoon figures to illustrate what Robert de Courcon thought a university lecturer ought to be like, and what Jacques de Vitry thought they were really like.

3 In groups, draw up simple questions to use in a 'grammar match', first in English, then in a foreign language that you learn (for example the past tense of verbs like 'buy', 'have', 'catch', 'go', 'swim').

SAINTS AND SUPERSTITION

Saints in the Christian church are those very few people who have led such holy lives that they have reached heaven without having to suffer in Purgatory (see page 7). Medieval Christians believed that the saints' closeness to God gave them special powers to ask God to forgive the sins of the living. The Christian church continually emphasized that although you might approach God through the saints and ask them to speak to God on your behalf, you must never worship the saints themselves, and certainly not their images, as the second of the Ten Commandments (Rules believed to have been given by God to Moses) forbids this. But many people found it more comfortable to pray to the saints, whom they thought of as friendly and approachable, real people like they were themselves. They prayed to painted or carved images of the saints and *martyrs* (people who had died for their beliefs) despite the Second

Commandment. They were still finding it hard to adjust to the idea that there was only one god, and still thought of the saints in the same way that, for example, ancient Greeks or Romans thought about the gods of mythology.

A thirteenth century book called the *Golden Legend*, which told the stories of the saints' lives, was used by artists to give them ideas for their paintings and carvings. The saints were always represented with their own 'attributes' or symbols, so that people who could not read could identify which saint was which. For example, St Catherine, who was a Christian scholar torn to pieces on a wheel for her beliefs and then executed, is shown with a book, a sword or a wheel. St Barbara, who was imprisoned in a tower by her father, who then killed her, is shown with a tower. St John the Baptist is shown barefoot, with a staff, often wearing an animal skin.

This fifteenth century painting by Pisanello shows St Eustace, who was a Roman general. He saw a vision of a stag with a crucifix in its antlers, became a Christian, and was martyred by burning. His attributes are a stag, a crucifix, and an oven.

An illustration from a thirteenth century manuscript showing the shrine of St Edward the Confessor at Westminster Abbey.

Christians associated different powers with different saints. St Sebastian and St Roch were believed to be able to heal plague victims; St Christopher was believed to be able to protect travellers. Eventually people began to believe that even a glance at an image of St Christopher would keep them safe for the rest of the day, and that a saint who could heal a particular disease could also inflict it, for example St Anthony was blamed for inflammations, and St Maur for gout.

This crossed the border between true Christian belief and superstitious belief in magic. The medieval church was full of superstitious beliefs and practices. Another belief was that *relics* (physical remains) of saints and martyrs (and also holy men called confessors, and holy virgins) could bring people closer to God, or had miraculous or magic powers of healing. An Abbot in France in the twelfth century claimed that the body of a holy man buried in his church could cure, amongst other things, deafness, blindness, insanity, tumours and jaundice – not to speak of toothache and spots.

People were so eager to get hold of holy relics that they would go to bizarre lengths to do so. One man is said to have bitten off pieces of the arm bone of the dead St Mary Magdalen; a group of peasants in Italy tried to kill a holy *hermit* (someone who lived by himself) so that they would be first on the scene to collect relics.

Many – if not most – relics were not really what they were supposed to be, for example drops of the Virgin Mary's breast milk and pieces of the cross on which Jesus had been nailed. If all the pieces of the 'True Cross' had been put together, they would have made not just a cross or a tree but a whole wood. The English poet Geoffrey Chaucer describes someone with some false relics in the fourteenth century like this:

> 'In his trunk he had a pillow-case
> Which he asserted was Our Lady's veil.
> He said he had a gobbet [piece] of the sail
> Saint Peter had, the time when he made bold
> To walk the waves, till Jesus Christ took hold.'

In churches, relics were kept in special boxes called *reliquaries*, often on stone bases high up in churches often above the altar, where they would be safer from people who might steal them. The places where they were kept were called shrines. Shrines attracted visitors who came on pilgrimages to see them (see pages 28–31).

SAINTS AND SUPERSTITION

Impatient patients

This is an account of the behaviour of the crowds who flocked to the church of St Pierre-sur-Dives in Normandy in 1145, expecting to be cured, but not receiving their wish.

If their cure was delayed and they did not immediately obtain what they desired, they stripped off their clothes and lay on the ground naked from the loins upwards, forgetting all shame, men, women and children together; and thus stretched on the ground, they crawled not on hands and knees but clawed with their whole bodies to the high altar.

What phrase in the account suggests that the writer did not approve of the behaviour he was describing?

A medieval woodcut showing a miraculous cure. How can you tell that the healer is both a bishop and a saint? What do you think the little demon symbolizes?

THINGS TO DO

1 From an encyclopaedia, find out more about the stories of the saints, starting with those mentioned on pages 24–25, and then going on to St Sebastian, St Jerome, St Ursula, St Agnes, and St George.

2 The saints' attributes reminded people what was important about the life of each saint. If you were a medieval painter what attributes would you use for a portrait of your mother, father, or other relative? What about the Prime Minister, the President of the USA, or your favourite singer or sportsperson?

3 Draw a picture, diagram or cartoon of one of the saints you have read about. You could show the saint with his or her attribute, or tell the story of a famous event in his or her life (like the picture of St Christopher opposite.) Use words on your work to explain it if necessary.

CHECK YOUR UNDERSTANDING

What is meant by:

martyr
relic
shrine
hermit

A dog saint

The legend of St Roch tells how the saint's dog fetched him food every day when he had caught the plague from plague sufferers he had been helping in Italy. But when the saint recovered and went home, he could not stop the people of Montpellier (in France) where he lived, from locking up the dog, who died. The dog became popularly known as St Guinefort, the dog martyr, and is often included in pictures of St Roch.

Q

Was the dog really like a saint or martyr?

A woodcut of 1423 which shows St Christopher carrying the Christ child across a stream. (Some people even today wear St Christopher medallions, to keep them safe on journeys.)

A fifteenth century hospital

CAN YOU REMEMBER ?

Which set of rules used by Christians forbids the worship of images?
What the character in Chaucer said was 'our Lady's Veil'?
Which saints were thought to be able to heal plague victims?
Which saint was imprisoned in a tower by her father?

A manuscript illustration showing St James himself on the journey to his own shrine. You can see the cockleshell symbol (see page 29) on his hat and his bag.

The medieval church taught that people should confess their sins to a priest. If they were truly sorry, then God would forgive their sins. But they would suffer for them in Purgatory when they died, and they might also be given a *penance* (an earthly punishment) by the priest, such as saying a number of psalms. For really serious sins, the priest might order people to go on a pilgrimage (journey to a holy place) where they would visit a shrine. They might have to wear special clothes to indicate that they were on the pilgrimage as a penance, or chains if they had killed someone. They would have to report to different monasteries or priests on the way, and when they arrived they might have to perform a further punishment, such as kneeling in ice-cold water to say their prayers. Sometimes people were sentenced to an everlasting pilgrimage, which was a kind of exile and meant that they could never come home again.

Some people went on pilgrimages voluntarily, maybe to give thanks for recovery from a disease, or perhaps because they had made a vow or promised a dying relative that they would do so. For people who were rich and adventurous enough, it was just a way of seeing foreign places. These pilgrims did not usually wear special clothes except big brimmed hats, often pinned at the front with badges bought at shrines visited on previous pilgrimages. So in some ways pilgrims were just medieval tourists; pilgrimages became very commercialized, and were quite an important part of the medieval economy. Sea-captains made a good living from ferrying pilgrims from Italy to the Holy Land. On the roads leading to shrines people could make money by providing accommodation and selling food and drink. At the shrine, you were often charged a fee to see the holy relic, so the church or monastery which owned it became quite rich. The money gained might then be spent on more paintings, sculpture, stained glass windows, silver and gold plate or embroidered hangings or altar-cloths. Pilgrims therefore indirectly helped to support the craftsmen and women who made these goods.

One of the most famous shrines in Western Europe was the shrine of St James at Compostela in Spain. There were stall-holders around the cathedral where the shrine was kept, selling leather bags, purses and slippers and changing currency, much as they still do today. Some sold the cockleshells which became famous as souvenirs of St James' shrine and served as evidence of a visit. Inside the cathedral a huge incense-holder was built which could be swung up and down the nave to fumigate it (freshen the air) – very necessary since all the poor pilgrims who could not afford hostels would just camp out there.

Beggars and the homeless sometimes took advantage of the fact that it was thought to be a Christian act of charity to give food and drink to passing pilgrims. At Compostela they would find a cockleshell and join the pilgrims in order to be given free provisions. An act of Parliament was passed in England towards the end of the thirteenth century which said that pilgrims had to carry identification, otherwise they could be arrested. Sometimes violence broke out amongst pilgrim bands.

As an alternative penance to going on a pilgrimage, a fashion developed in the thirteenth century for people to wander about in bands singing psalms and lashing themselves with whips. They said this was a punishment for not just their sins but the sins of the whole world, believing that they could get closer to God by imitating the suffering of Jesus. They thought that by undergoing punishment now they might avoid some of the worse punishment due to them on Judgment Day, when God would give them their just deserts. These people were called *flagellants*, which means people who beat themselves. The first flagellants came from Italy, but the movement quickly spread Northwards. Some German flagellants in 1261 claimed to have a letter from heaven, a copy of a message read out by an angel from a tablet written by God which said that humanity could have one last chance of forgiveness if another flagellant procession was organized.

The flagellants were seen by the authorities in both the church and the state as a threat to ordered society, and they tried to prevent the processions, but without much success. The flagellants flourished, becoming more hostile to the church and seizing church property. They became increasingly hysterical in their behaviour, mugging and killing Jews and clergy.

An illustration from a manuscript of John Lydgate's poems showing pilgrims leaving Canterbury for the Holy Land. How wealthy do you think these travellers are?

Indulgences

By far the easiest kind of punishment for sin for people who had money was to pay a fine to the church in return for an *indulgence* (pardon). Originally the indulgence just excused your earthly punishment or penance; you would still be punished in Purgatory. But eventually the church was selling indulgences to cover your punishment in Purgatory too. There was no real Christian justification for this idea. Indulgences were sold by Pardoners, who, while handing over some of the money to the church, somehow also managed to get quite rich themselves.

Educational journeys

I say of a truth, that in forty weeks of this pilgrimage people learn to know themselves better than in forty years elsewhere. And we see with our own eyes at the present day that mere laymen, with no knowledge of the Holy Scriptures, after they have made a pilgrimage to the holy places and have returned, argue about the Gospel and the prophets, talk upon theological subjects, and sometimes overcome and set right learned divines in their interpretation of difficult passages of Holy Scripture, because no Catholic returns from there without having become more learned.

(From the writings of Felix Faber, a 15th century German)

What kinds of knowledge could people acquire on a pilgrimage?

The church at Santiago de Compostela, which houses the shrine of St James. Santiago is the Spanish for St James.

THINGS TO DO

1 Using the information on pages 28–29 and the poem and extract on pages 30–31, write an extract from the diary of a pilgrim, recording what you are most afraid of on your pilgrimage, and what you hope to gain.

2 Write a list of what medieval pilgrims would need to take with them, explaining how they would carry it all, and whether they would be likely to bring exactly the same things home.

A fifteenth century drawing of a group of German flagellants from the Constance Chronicles. The writing you can see above the figures is in an old form of German – the actual language used by many flagellants instead of the Latin used by the Catholic Church.

Embarking on a pilgrimage

This early fifteenth century poem is about English pilgrims setting sail for Spain to visit the shrine of St James at Compostela.

> Men may leave all games
> That sail to St James
> For many a man it grames [grieves]
> When they begin to sail
> For when they have taken the sea
> At Sandwich or at Winchelsea
> At Bristol or where that it be
> Their hearts begin to fail.

Sea-voyages

This story was told to Jacques de Vitry in the thirteenth century,

> **Certain abominable traitors, having received payment to furnish the pilgrims with provisions right to their port of destination, have stocked their ships with only a little meat, and then, after a few days' journey, have starved their pilgrims to death and cast them ashore on an island, or (most cruel of all) have sold them as manservants to the Saracens (Arabs).**

Q

Whereabouts in England are the ports that they sailed from? Which of the three is still an important port today?

Which shrine could they have visited near Sandwich and Winchelsea without having to go to sea?

Why do you think their hearts began to fail?

CHECK YOUR UNDERSTANDING

What is meant by the following?

penance
flagellant
indulgence
Saracen

CAN YOU REMEMBER ?

*Why a priest might tell someone to go on a pilgrimage?
What badges the pilgrims who had been to Compostela wore?
What dangers pilgrims might meet on their way?
Why pilgrims in England had to carry identification?*

In the Middle Ages the only public building big enough for a large number of people to get together in was the church. The only place where you could look at pictures or any kind of image was the church. So people saw churches as exciting places, where they could enjoy themselves at holiday times, as well as solemn places where they went to worship.

Everybody had *holidays* (holidays just means holy days, when people did not have to work) at the same time. There were big holiday festivities in and around the church, depending on the time of year; Christmas Games, May Games, Rogation Games (held in late spring or early summer), Midsummer Games, and Whitsun and Harvest feasting and drinking. People carried evergreen holly into the church at Christmas, and new spring leaves at Easter. On May Day they built arbours and bowers (shelters) of greenery against the outside of the church. The church was the natural place for celebration, and people liked to decorate it for holidays as you might decorate somewhere for a party.

Most of the Christian holidays of medieval times had grown out of the *pagan* (non-Christian) celebrations of the *solstices* (longest and shortest days of the year) and the *equinoxes* (when day and night are equal in spring and autumn). At these times people prayed that the land and their animals would be fertile and their crops abundant. Agricultural fertility was associated in people's minds with human fertility. Easter, which fell around the spring equinox was associated with new life and renewed growth. A thirteenth century priest in Cumbria encouraged his parishioners to join in a fertility dance as part of Easter celebrations, while he bore aloft on a pole before the dancers a representation of the human organs of reproduction.

In Sarum in Wiltshire a ceremony for blessing a huge Paschal Candle (a candle lit in churches just after Easter time) at the church font was symbolic in sexual as well as religious terms.

Another period of holidays and celebrations took place between the end of May and the end of June. In the Christian calendar this period was bounded by the Christian holidays of Ascension Day (40 days after Easter) and St John the Baptist's Day on 24 June, but it kept some of its links with the pagan Midsummer festival in which it originated. At the beginning of the period, *rogations* (processions through the fields to pray for the crops) were held. Everyone would join in, ringing bells and waving banners and garlands of milkwort (a countryside plant) to scare demons away from the new crops and make them fertile.

Some of the outdoor games and celebrations at these church festivals were those people still enjoy today – football, javelin throwing, archery and wrestling. Among those you don't see today were

cock-fighting and leaping over rolling flame wheels. Hobby horses in the shape of stick horses or horse skulls were often kept in churches and brought out at holiday times. Riders would caper around on them making people laugh and collecting money. A more sinister custom was the wearing of beast heads and frightening people in the dark.

It was also popular at different holiday times to crown a 'summer king' or 'May queen', or at Christmas a 'boy bishop' or 'lord of misrule'. These were ordinary people who were set up in mock authority for the holiday. They would make their own rules allowing things which were normally forbidden, and overturning normal authority. Sometimes the joke got out of hand, particularly if people had been drinking, and it was difficult to restore order again. The custom was still going on in the sixteenth century. Phillip Stubbes in *The Anatomie of Abuses* published in 1583 described how a king of misrule and his company marched to the church to interrupt the service

'their pipers piping, their drummers thundering, their bells jingling, their handkerchiefs swinging about their heads like madmen, their hobby horses and other monsters skirmishing amongst the route.'

The Fight between Carnival and Lent by Pieter (the Elder) Brueghel. Although this painting was painted in the 16th century, a little later than the medieval period, it shows the kind of festivities medieval people probably had. Lent is the forty days before Easter, when people fasted, and Carnival was originally a name for the days before Lent when they ate up all the meat left over after the winter. The fight between Carnival and Lent is a symbol of indulgence struggling with self-control.

Lay fraternities

In some remote areas of Europe there were very few local priests and the work they might have done was done instead by *lay fraternities*, which were associations people joined for religious purposes. 'Lay' refers to people who are not clergymen, and 'fraternity' means 'brotherhood'. The members of the fraternities thought that by clubbing together to raise money and do Christian acts, they might save their immortal souls. By the later Middle Ages, fraternities were popular in towns and villages as well. Some fraternity members visited sick people or set up hospitals, some helped the poor by giving them money, or taking responsibility for seeing to the burial of those who had no family or whose families could not afford it. Others took responsibility for repairing and rebuilding churches. Something like one fifth of the adult population of Europe may have belonged to fraternities at the height of their popularity.

This illustration from the Luttrell Psalter (written in the fourteenth century) shows people enjoying themselves in a scene familiar today – a 'piggy-back' fight.

THINGS TO DO

1 Make a poster advertising a medieval day of Midsummer Games, giving information about the events to be held, their location, and other festivities.

2 In groups of three or four, draw up the statement of a medieval Lord of Misrule, saying what people are allowed to do for the period of the holiday that they would not normally be allowed to do. Draw up a similar statement of a Lord – or Lady – of Misrule in your history class. Remember in both cases that if things get too unruly, someone puts a stop to the proceedings.

3 Find out about what the *Round Table*, the *Rotary Club* and the *Lions* do today. What similarities are there with the medieval fraternities? Are there any important differences?

4 Sketch out a calendar showing the months of the year, and highlight the holiday times when Medieval people would look forward to festivities. Add any saint's days that you can find out. How do these holiday periods compare with yours?

CAN YOU REMEMBER ?

The origins of the word 'holiday'?
What sports were popular in medieval times?
What pagan customs found their way into the Christian way of life?
The purpose of lay fraternities?

Wrestling in Clerkenwell

To our Lord the King. The poor Prioress of Clerkenwell prays that he will to provide and order a remedy because the people of London lay waste and destroy her corn and grass by their miracle plays and wrestling matches, so that she has no profit of them nor can have unless the king have pity, for they are a savage folk and we cannot stand against them and cannot get justice by any law.

(Public Record Office, Ancient Petition 4858)

Q

If you look on an up to date road atlas or map of London, you can see where Clerkenwell is. Why do you think Londoners went to Clerkenwell to hold their wrestling and plays? Why couldn't the Prioress stop them?

This manuscript shows children riding hobby horses, a game which probably had pagan origins.

Never on Sunday

No servile works shall be done on Sundays, neither shall men perform their rustic labours, tending vines, ploughing fields, reaping corn and mowing hay, setting up hedges or fencing woods, cutting trees or working in quarries or building houses; nor shall they work in the garden, nor come to the law courts, nor follow the chase. Also women shall not do their textile works, nor cut out clothes, nor stitch them together with the needle, nor card wool, nor beat hemp, nor wash clothes in public, nor shear sheep: so that there may be rest on the Lord's day.

(Frankish decree of 827)

Q

Why do you think the Church forbade these activities on Sundays? What did the clergy want people to do instead?
Are there any 'rustic (country) labours' which are not mentioned here, which *would* have been allowed?
Some of the activities here might be thought of as leisure activities today. Which are they? Can you explain why ideas about them have changed?

CHECK YOUR UNDERSTANDING

What do the following mean?

solstice
pagan
rogations
lay

CHRISTIAN ART AND DRAMA

Most medieval people could not read, so the only way they could find out anything was by listening to other people or looking at pictures. This is how they learned about Christian teaching. Inside a church building, apart from listening to the priest's sermons, you could find a whole array of visual representations of Christian stories and ideas. Even in the smallest churches there would be paintings of scenes from the life of Jesus and the Virgin Mary, such as the *Annunciation* (the angel Gabriel telling Mary she would have a son), the Nativity and the Crucifixion. These scenes might be painted on the wall, or on wood panels over the altar, and might appear too in stained glass windows if the church were rich enough to have them. Images made the stories vivid and memorable, and often aroused deeply emotional religious feelings such as love for the baby Jesus or pity for the crucified Christ.

People might feel terrified by representations of the torments of hell (like the one on page 39) or overwhelmed with gratitude that God would forgive sinners who were truly sorry for what they had done.

Drama was used in church too. The clergy dramatized parts of the Mass and other services, which were all said or sung in Latin. At Christmas the dramatized part of the service became a brief Nativity play performed by the priests, and at Easter, a play about the Resurrection of Jesus. In the later Middle Ages a custom grew up of putting on plays in the towns. The plays told Bible stories about the whole history of humanity in relation to God, going back to the Creation, the Fall of Adam and Eve, and God's punishment of sinful people by the Flood. Another sombre play was about the Day of

Judgment when God administered punishment for sins, but on the whole the tone was humorous. More cheerful stories would tell how Christ bought God's forgiveness of people's sins by his death and resurrection. Often, one of the characters was God; in the box on the right God tells Noah to build his Ark.

The plays were called Mystery or Miracle Plays in England, because they dealt with the hidden truths and marvels about God. They are now often called Corpus Christi plays because they came to be performed on the holiday of Corpus Christi, which means the body of Christ, a new holiday set up in 1264 to be celebrated on the first Thursday after Trinity Sunday. This would usually fall in June so it added to the Midsummer festivities. The plays were organised by the *civic* (town) authorities and

> Therefore Noah, my servant free,
> That righteous man art, as I see
> A ship soon thou shalt make thee
> Of trees dry and light.
> Little chambers therein thou make;
> And binding pitch also thou take.
>
> Eating-places thou make also,
> Three-roofed chambers on a row;
> For with water I think to flow
> Man that I did make
> Destroyed all the world shall be
> Save thou, thy wife, thy sons three
> And all their wives also with thee
> Shall saved be for they sake.
>
> (From the *Chester Pageant*)

performed by members of the *guilds*, which were groups responsible for standards and employment in the crafts and trades. Those which put on plays included the carpenters, pewterers, cooks and innkeepers, coopers (who made barrels and buckets) and tailors. It was usual for the clergy to have a hand in writing down the words of the plays, and directing them. This meant that they could make sure that the interpretation of the Bible stories stuck more or less to official church teaching. No doubt the clergy approved of people spending their day off not just having fun but also thinking about God and Jesus Christ.

In Germany, people put on *Passion plays*, which dealt with the last days in the life of Jesus, and his execution. (Passion is a word for suffering.)

A thirteenth century church painting by Margarito of Arezzo, which shows Mary surrounded by scenes from the lives of the saints. Which two of Mary's roles does he show? Can you see St Benedict, who wrote the 'Very little rule for beginners' (see page 13) rolling in brambles to conquer his sinful thoughts, and St Margaret, who was swallowed by a dragon?

CHRISTIAN ART AND DRAMA

A mystery play about Abraham and Isaac

This is an extract from a play which was probably performed regularly in Chester. It tells the Old Testament story of how Abraham was told by God to sacrifice his son Isaac, but at the last minute was stopped by an angel. The extract is spoken by Isaac when he really believes his father is going to kill him.

> Nay, nay father, God forbid
> That ever you should grieve Him, for me.
> You have other children, one or two,
> Which ye should love well by kind [by nature].
> I pray you, father, make you no woe;
> For, once I be dead and from you go,
> I shall be soon out of your mind.
> Therefore do our Lord's bidding,
> And when I am dead, then pray for me.
> But good father, tell ye my mother nothing;
> Say that I am in another country dwelling.

Mystery plays usually contained religious or semi-religious messages about how people should behave, as well as telling Bible stories. This extract suggests what family relationships between parents and children should be like. Does it seem to you to be a realistic view?

A fourteenth century illustration of a miracle play about a martyr suffering death for her faith.

THINGS TO DO

1 Translate God's commands to Noah on page 37 into modern English. 'Flow' in line 9 means 'drown'.
2 Find some old Christmas cards with reproductions of religious paintings. Find the date of the paintings to see if any of them were painted in the medieval period. What do they tell or remind you about Christian teaching?

CAN YOU REMEMBER ?

How most ordinary medieval people found out about Christian beliefs?
Why the clergy liked to get involved in putting on plays?
Which different tradespeople joined in putting on plays?
Which towns in England had their own plays to put on?

CHECK YOUR UNDERSTANDING

What do the following words mean?

guilds
coopers
civic
Annunciation
Corpus Christi

The richness of church art

William of Malmesbury, a twelfth century monk, described how people wanted everything inside their churches to look splendid.

> We think it not enough in our holy vessels (containers) unless the heavy metal (gold) is eclipsed by precious stones; by the flame of the topaz, the violet of the amethyst, the green of the emerald; unless there is a riot of gold in the priestly vestments (garments) and unless the walls glisten with multicoloured paintings and reflect the sunlight right up to the ceiling.

These riches were usually funded by rich people who gave money to the church, or left it to the church in their wills, in return for Masses to be said for their souls.

Why were the riches of the church usually safe from thieves?
Why did people leave money to the church rather than their families?
What do you think became of all these riches?

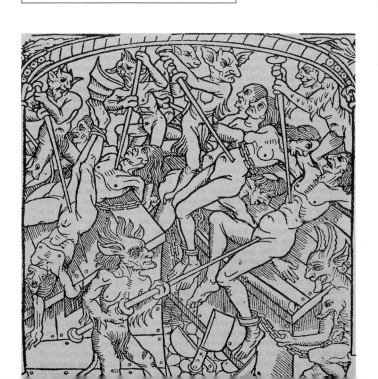

Putting on a Mystery play

The following descriptions about the performance of Mystery plays come from the sixteenth and early seventeenth centuries, but little had changed since medieval times, so they give a fairly accurate picture of how the plays would have been put on in the Middle Ages. Read the two descriptions and then draw a cartoon or diagram showing a) your idea of what the 'pageant' or wheeled carriage on which the plays were performed looked like, and b) how the actors playing Adam, Eve and God would have looked in their costumes. A 'coat' in the Middle Ages meant a long-sleeved gown.

> This pageant or carriage was a high place made like a house with two rooms, being open on the top; In the lower room they apparelled [clothed] and dressed themselves, and in the higher room they played; and they stood upon six wheels.
>
> (*Description of a Chester 'pageant'* David Rogers, *The Breviary of Chester History*, 1609)

> A rib coloured red
> 2 coats and a pair hosen for Eve, stained
> A coat and hosen for Adam, stained
> A face [mask] and hair [wig] for the Father
> 2 hairs for Adam and Eve
>
> (Props for *The Creation of Eve*, Inventory of the Norwich Grocers' Company, 1565)

This woodcut shows the torments of Hell. How are the devils tormenting the sinners? Can you see evidence to suggest that the artist thought that even monks might go to Hell?

A manuscript showing women being seduced away from the true faith by male heretics.

Almost everything people did in the Middle Ages was influenced by the church. The church determined when they worked and when they had a holiday. The church told them how they ought to behave. When they gave money to a beggar or food to a pilgrim it was because the church said it was a Christian thing to do. When they stole or lied or committed adultery they felt guilty because the church told them these things were wrong. If they swore or blasphemed against God, or even uttered the curious Flemish oath, 'I deny boots' (Je renie de bottes) – which was a way of *not* denying God – they might feel defiant rather than guilty, but they would be conscious that what they were defying was the church. The church had something to say about every situation. You always knew what you ought to do, and you knew that if you failed to do it you should confess to the priest, who would both decide your earthly punishment and warn you of more punishment to come after death. Because of the belief in the afterlife, the church had tremendous psychological control over people. It was able to reassure them of future bliss in Heaven, or cast them into anxiety with threats of everlasting torment.

The church was also very rich, getting money in a variety of ways. The clergy emphasised that dead souls could be relieved of some time in Purgatory by the saying of Masses. Masses could only be said by the clergy themselves, and they charged money for saying them. They told rich people that they could help their own souls after death by leaving their money to the church or by providing a painting or other work of art. And monasteries and the great cathedrals owned vast areas of land which they rented out for a large income, or farmed profitably themselves. All this required efficient administration, and the church, with its control of education, could always find able administrators.

So the church was the single most rich and powerful institution in Europe. In order to protect its wealth and power it developed an extensive and effective authority structure. At the head of the church was the Pope, who was chosen for life. His authority was delegated via archbishops and bishops to the parish priests all over Europe, who were able to exert control over ordinary people.

One potential challenge to the church was the development of different beliefs, which could lead people to resist the church in other areas too. The church authorities were determined not to lose their power through this kind of fragmentation. They also believed that only true belief could save a soul from hell. So anyone who deviated from the *orthodox* (standard) belief of the church was called a heretic, and could be disciplined. If you believed that Jesus was wholly man, not God and man at once, or that God the Father had existed before God the Son, or that there was a force of evil at large in the world which was nearly as strong as God's goodness, then you were a heretic, and subject to the *Inquisition*, which was an organization set up in 1232 for enforcing orthodoxy. The Inquisitors tried to root out heretics at any cost; fair or unfair means were used equally. People thought to be heretics were questioned without knowing what they were charged with, then tortured, and if this failed they were asked a series of questions to which they were guaranteed not to know the answers. Not surprisingly the Inquisitors were widely feared and hated.

The clergy could also discipline people who refused to conform by *excommunicating* them. This meant excluding them from the sacraments and preventing them, if they died, from having a Christian burial. The effectiveness of this kind of discipline depended on the effectiveness of the church teaching to which those disciplined had previously been exposed. If they really believed, as the church taught, that the sacraments brought you closer to God and that without them you would suffer torment after death, they might be frightened. But heretics by their very nature were independent thinkers. Very often excommunication had little effect.

In most countries the *secular ruler* (non-religious ruler such as a king or a duke) respected the Pope and worked together with the local bishops to make sure people lived orderly lives. The church and state authorities both benefited from social order, as those who have power over others always do. They are always conscious that rebellion will threaten their power. However, there were also some famous power struggles between church and state (see pages 42–43).

THE POWER OF THE CHURCH

The Church and Non-Christians

The two important groups of non-Christians in medieval Europe were the Muslims of Southern Spain and the Jews. The church encouraged the Christians in Spain to fight against the Muslim Moors and drive them out of the country. By the middle of the thirteenth century Muslims remained only in the Moorish kingdom of Granada at the southern tip of Spain.

But there were Jewish communities in most of the larger towns in Europe throughout the Middle Ages. There was a great deal of anti-Semitism (anti-Jewish feeling). Church teaching emphasized the role of the Jews in the crucifixion of Jesus and played down the fact that it was the Roman Pontius Pilate who made the decision to sentence Jesus to death. Popular belief therefore blamed the Jews for the crucifixion; people forgot that Jesus himself and most of the writers of the New Testament had been practising Jews. Plays like the German Passion Plays (see page 37) encouraged anti-Semitism. Although the church authorities defended the Jews' right to live among Christians, in many areas of Europe clergy and friars encouraged people to throw stones at Jews and attack their property. Jews were made to live in particular areas of the towns and cities, and to wear yellow badges or ribbons, or in some areas tall pointed hats for the men and veils for the women.

Hieronymus Bosch, a Flemish artist, painted this picture of Christ being mocked as he carries the cross very early in the sixteenth century. Some people see this as an anti-Semitic painting, because of the cartoon-like caricatures Bosch has used to portray the Jewish people here.

A Curse

A worse threat than excommunication was an anathema, or curse. In 1346 the Pope cursed King Louis of Bavaria, saying,

**Let him be damned in his going out and his coming in.
May the Lord strike him with madness and blindness.
May the wrath of the Omnipotent (all-powerful) burn itself into him in the present and future world.**

CAN YOU REMEMBER ?

*How the church made so much money?
Why the Inquisition was hated so much?*

Which part of the curse do you think the King would have found most disturbing?

A medieval illustration of Archbishop Thomas Becket being murdered in Canterbury Cathedral.

Papal Claims and Royal Challenges

We declare, assert, define and pronounce that it is entirely necessary for salvation that all human creation be subject to the pope of Rome.

(Papal Bull, Unam Sanctam, quoted in G.R. Elton, *Renaissance and Reformation, 1300–1648*)

The sentence above is part of a document published by Pope Boniface VIII in 1302. A few weeks afterwards he was captured and taken prisoner by King Philip IV of France, with whom he had been quarrelling about the King's power over the French clergy. Another famous quarrel between church and state took place when Thomas Becket, Archbishop of Canterbury in the reign of Henry II of England, refused to obey the King and the King had him murdered. He was made a martyr, and his shrine at Canterbury became a popular place for pilgrims. These two kings would probably not have agreed with Boniface VIII's idea that kings should be subject to the pope.

Why would Boniface VIII's idea be difficult to enforce?

THINGS TO DO

1 Devise an anathema which might persuade you to do what you were told when you didn't want to. You will need to think what you would mind most – it might be something physical like the madness and blindness in the Pope's curse, or it might be getting left out of the team or not being able to watch television.

Write out your anathema in the same kind of dramatic language the Pope used in the extract on page 42.

2 Both Christians and non-Christians might agree with some of the heretical beliefs described on page 41. Consider whether there are any that you find quite reasonable.

CHECK YOUR UNDERSTANDING

What do the following mean?

excommunication
anathema
secular
orthodox

What Can You Remember?

Why was the medieval church rich and powerful?

Why did medieval people spend so much time on religious activities?

How were people who could not read taught about Christian beliefs?

Why did people go on pilgrimages?

Who founded the first monasteries?

Why was it popular to become a monk or a nun?

Why were holiday festivities celebrated in and around the church?

Why are there still so many churches surviving from the Middle Ages?

Why were the Virgin Mary and the saints popular with ordinary people?

Why did medieval people spend their money building and decorating churches?

Study the picture above before answering the questions below.

Who is the artist portraying in the centre of the painting?

Comparing this picture with other paintings in the book, can you guess which century it was painted in?

This painting was paid for by a rich nobleman. What can you see in the picture that might give you clues about the way in which he lived?

Why do you think the nobleman might want a picture like this painted?

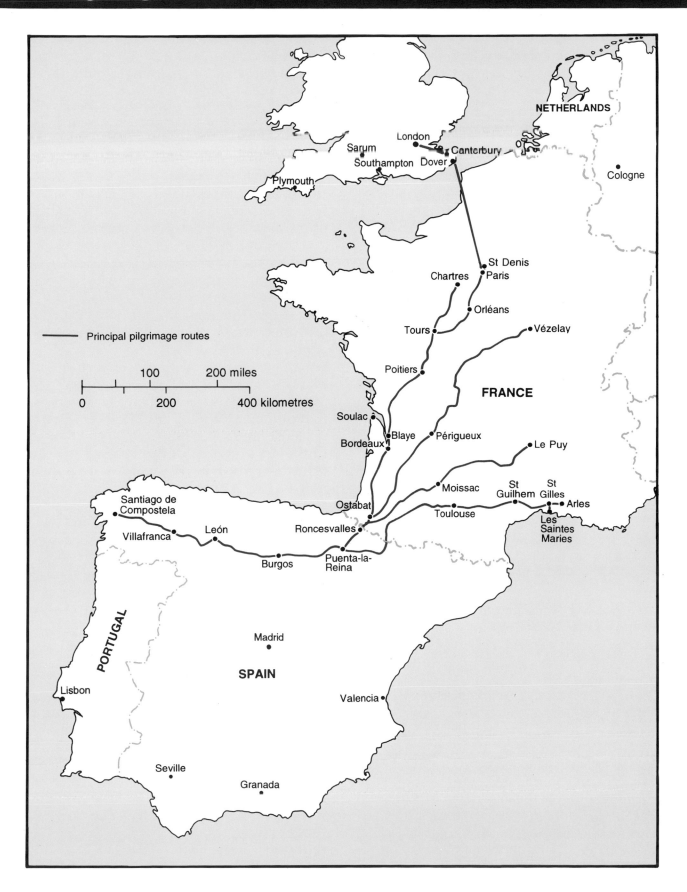

Principal pilgrimage routes

NETHERLANDS

Cologne

London
Sarum
Southampton
Dover
Canterbury
Plymouth

St Denis
Chartres
Paris
Orléans
Tours
Vézelay

FRANCE

Poitiers

Soulac
Blaye
Périgueux
Bordeaux
Le Puy

Moissac
St Guilhem
St Gilles
Arles
Toulouse
Les Saintes Maries
Ostabat

Santiago de Compostela
Villafranca
León
Roncesvalles
Burgos
Puenta-la-Reina

PORTUGAL

Madrid

SPAIN

Lisbon

Valencia

Seville

Granada

100   200 miles
0   200   400 kilometres

GLOSSARY

abbot   head of a monastery

absolution   sacrament in which people receive forgiveness for their sins after confessing to a priest

alms   charity

altar   holy table

anathema   curse

Annunciation   the announcement by the angel Gabriel to Mary that she would have a son

apparel   clothing

arbours and bowers   shelters made from greenery

Augustinians   order of monks founded by St Augustine

Benedictines   order of monks founded by St Benedict of Nursia

Beguine   a word for heretic, or for women living a communal religious life

bequests   property left in a will

blasphemy   speaking against God

chastity   living without sex

Cistercians   an order of monks founded at Citeaux in France

civic   to do with a town

clergy   people dedicated to religion, such as priests, bishops, monks, friars and nuns

confirmation   the sacrament for people to repeat the promises which their godparents made for them at their baptism

coopers   makers of barrels and buckets

cope   cloak

Dominicans   order of friars founded by St Dominic

dowry   property brought by a woman to her husband on marriage

equinoxes   when day and night are of equal length

Eucharist   name for the Mass

flagellants   people who beat themselves

font   basin used for baptism

Franciscans   order of friars founded by St Francis of Assisi

fumigate   freshen the air

Golden Legend   thirteenth-century book containing stories of the lives of saints

Gospels   four books of the New Testament

grace of God   God's help to people fighting sin

guilds   groups responsible for standards and employment in different crafts and trades

habits   religious clothing worn by monks, nuns and friars

heresy   beliefs different from the official beliefs of the Catholic church

heretic   people who believe in heresy

hermit   someone who lives in isolation away from other people

Holy Communion   a name for the Mass used in the Church of England

Holy Matrimony   the sacrament of marriage

Holy Unction   sacrament received by the dying

illumination   art of decorating manuscripts with pictures and designs

indulgence   pardon

Inquisition   church organization for enforcing standard beliefs

Last Rites   another name for Holy Unction

lay fraternities   religious associations for people who are not clergy

Lent   the forty days of fasting just before Easter

martyrs   people who die for their beliefs

Mass   Church service with bread and wine

metaphor   expressing meaning by making comparisons

milkwort   countryside plant

Miracle or Mystery plays   plays about miracles or hidden religious truths

mitre   pointed double hat worn by a bishop

omnipotent   all powerful

ordination   sacrament for making men into priests or bishops

orthodox   standard

Paschal candle   candle lit just after Easter

Passion plays   plays about the betrayal of Jesus and his crucifixion

penance   earthly punishment for sin

pewterers   craftsmen working in pewter

Poor Clares   order set up by women wanting to live in poverty

Pope   the head of the Roman Catholic church

prophet   someone who predicts the future

prophecy   prediction

psalm   religious poem or song from the Old Testament

Purgatory   condition of suffering before a soul entered Heaven

relics   physical remains

reliquary   container for relics

rhetoric   using language in set ways to express ideas and persuade people
rogations   processions through the fields to pray for the crops
Saracen   Arab
sacraments   symbols of God's help to people fighting sin
secular   non-religious
shrine   place where relics were kept

solstices   longest and shortest days of the year
symbolism   one thing representing another
Ten Commandments   rules believed to have been given by God to Moses
theologians   scholars who study religion
theology   study of religion
tithes   tax paid to the church of a tenth of people's produce
worsted   expensive woollen cloth

FINDING OUT MORE

For younger readers

Jane Sayers, *Life in a Mediaeval Monastery*, Longman.
Marjorie Reeves, *The Mediaeval Monastery*, Longman.
Kathleen Norman, *The Rise of Christian Europe*, Macmillan.
Alan Kendall, *Mediaeval Pilgrims*, Wayland.
Peter and Mary Speed, *The Church (The Middle Ages, Book 2)*, Oxford University Press.
Stig Hadenius and Birgit Janrup, *How they lived in a Mediaeval Monastery*, Butterworth.

For older readers

R. W. Southern, *Western society and the Church in the Middle Ages*, Hodder.
Boris Ford, *The Cambridge Cultural History (Mediaeval Britain)*, Cambridge University Press.
Andrew McCall, *The Mediaeval Underworld*, Dorset.

Places to visit

There are a lot of medieval cathedrals, churches and abbeys still in daily use in Europe. If you are on holiday abroad, try the local tourist information office to find out about old cathedrals or churches in the area. In Britain there are a huge number of medieval churches (or churches with medieval parts to them) in towns and villages, but the following are especially worth a visit: most cathedrals, particularly Canterbury (Kent), York, Salisbury (Wiltshire), Lincoln and Wells (Somerset); Rievaulx Abbey, Whitby Abbey, Fountains Abbey, Kirkham Priory and Byland Abbey (North Yorkshire); Westminster Abbey in London; Jarrow Priory (Tyne and Wear); Glastonbury Abbey (Somerset); Battle Abbey (Sussex); Holy Trinity Church in Long Melford, Suffolk; college chapels in Oxford and Cambridge; the Church of St Andrew, Norwich; and Southwell Minster, Nottinghamshire.

Acknowledgements

The author and publishers would like to thank the following for their permission to reproduce illustrations: Ronald Sheriden Ancient Art and Architecture Collection for pages 13, 14, 27 (bottom) and 30; Biblioteque National, Paris for page 21 (bottom); Bodleian Library for pages 21 (top), 23, 35 and 40; Bridgeman Art Library for pages 32–33; British Library for pages 4, 12, 28 and 34; Cambridge University Library for page 24; Michael Holford for page 29; Hulton Picture Library for page 26; Koninklijk Museum, Antwerp, for page 6; Mansell Collection for pages 11, 31, 38, 39 and 43; National Gallery for pages 1, 9, 17, 19, 25, 36–37 and 44; Foto Scala, Florence for page 5; Trinity College, Cambridge for page 20; the Dean and Chapter of Winchester for page 22; and to Ken Smith for drawing the maps and diagrams on pages 14 and 45.

Thanks go to the How It Was series editors for advice and editorial input: Madeline Jones and Michael Rawcliffe.

INDEX